PETER C. CAVELTI

Thoughtful Giving

Copyright © 2024 by the Author

The digital version of this book may be shared with and transmitted to others, provided its contents remain in their original and unabridged form.

A hard copy of this book is available for sale online and in book stores.

Any reproduction of the book's content, in its digital or hard-copy form, requires prior written permission by the Author. Quotations from the book are permitted with proper attribution.

The publisher is not responsible for websites or their content unless they are owned by the publisher.

ISBN 978-1-7780316-6-3 (paper)

ISBN 978-1-7780316-7-0 (digital)

Library and Archives of Canada

Cavelti, Peter C. (Peter Christian), 1948-

Thoughtful Giving: A Journey Through the Charitable Universe / Peter C. Cavelti

Cover and Content Design:

Minh Nguyen

Richard Moore Associates, New York, Hanoi and Saigon

Cover illustration from Pixabay

ALSO BY PETER C. CAVELTI

Tuiavii's Way: A South Sea Chief's Comments on Western Society

Legacy Editions, Toronto and Sanseido, Tokyo

A Dangerous Remedy

Legacy Editions, Toronto

Moments In Time: The Experience of my Life

Legacy Editions, Toronto

How To Invest In Gold

McClelland & Stewart, Toronto and Follett Publishing, Chicago

Gold, Silver & Strategic Metals

McClelland & Stewart, Toronto and McGraw Hill, New York

07	**Introduction**
	What Is Charity? *(The Lemonade Stand and the Refugee Camp)*
11	
19	**Epiphany** *(The Friday Visit that Helped Me Understand)*
	The Many Faces of Charity *(Frank's Approach and Other Popular Delusions)*
27	
37	**The Family Foundation** *(What I Learned from My Grandchildren)*
	Navigating the Charitable Map *(Thoughts about Human Failures and Hopes for a Better Future)*
47	
57	**The Good, the Bad and the Ugly** *(Three Easy Steps to Avoid Supporting Zombie Charities)*

How Many Causes Should We Support?   67
(Why We Cut the Number of Favoured Charities)

73   Operating Charities and "Public Foundations"
(Why Do I Need an Intermediary?)

A Donor's Rights   79
(Honouring a Donor's Rights Means Being Accountable)

87   Balancing Intention with Thought
(Back to Basics: the Challenge Is to Give Well)

Annex   91
A List of Charity Rating Services
A list of Insightful Educational Articles

99   Acknowledgements

Introduction

Let me start this guide with a bold statement. The vast majority of charities are poorly managed and don't put nearly enough of the funds they receive toward their stated goal. And when they do, it's often not in a timely or impactful manner.

As I frequently say to the people soliciting donations, "If your cause is as worthy and pressing as you say, why don't you put more of the grants you receive to work right away?" You'd think my question would be met by a long moment of silence, but that is rarely the case. Typically, the caller is perfectly familiar with such objections and politely ends the conversation. After all, staff members have no control over policy decisions. How much is spent on fundraising, administration and management salaries is decided in the executive suite.

I'm not one of Warren Buffett's fervent fans, but some of his comments about philanthropy deeply resonate. This one sums it all up: "Giving away money is easy. Giving money away well is fiendishly difficult."

In this series of essays I will reflect on my own journey through the charitable universe and explain how you can be sure that your gestures of kindness will not be in vain. After all, there are exceptionally efficient and impactful charities out there. Once you find them you'll know that your gifts make a difference. Instead of dwelling on the world's misery, you'll focus on what is possible!

What Is Charity?

The Lemonade Stand and the Refugee Camp

When the conversation turns to charity, many people join in with memories of their childhood days. "Yup, we used to have a lemonade stand on summer weekends, raising money for cancer research." Then they proudly add, "Now my kids do the same thing—except we adults have to make the lemonade."

When I grew up in rural post-war Europe the meaning of charitable giving was quite different. Where there was need, people helped each other. The universe of charitable organizations was far smaller than it is today. My father, a young dentist then, often came home with a crate of apples or a couple of hams—things he'd been given by farmers who couldn't pay their bills. My mom didn't like that and sometimes called him a bad businessman, but then quickly revised her narrative when she noticed we children were listening. Looking after the less fortunate, we were told, was an imperative.

At Christmas time, our mother sat down at the kitchen table and wrote notes to those she felt needed help: the Franciscan monks, the Dominican nuns, the Swiss Red Cross, the Institute for the Blind and the Salvation Army. She placed a ten-franc bill in each envelope and a postage stamp on the outside. As economic conditions improved and my father achieved unexpected success with his practice, the pile of Christmas envelopes and the amount of money they contained grew. The causes my parents eventually supported included a bird sanctuary, cancer research, programs for disabled children and numerous others.

In my early twenties, when backpacking around the world on something like ten dollars a day, I experienced a completely different face of charity. Here is a page from my battered travel journal:

> *The camp outside the city is said to accommodate more than half a million refugees and is serviced by a staff of 400. I join the short line-up of visitors wanting to get in, present my credentials, and get a piece of paper showing my name and passport number in Western characters, alongside numerous other notations in Hindi. As I enter, I'm intimidated by the vast ocean of canvas and cloth I see, most of it in shades of beige, brown, grey or green, suspended by a variety of ropes and wooden stakes. I first conclude that*

a huge logistical effort must have made this possible. Then I change my mind: more likely, this all started with a thousand tents, probably supplied by the Indian army, and when by day three or so tents were no longer available, every thinkable substitute was brought in, in a chaotic effort to give the desperate masses streaming in each day some token form of shelter.

The front line of tent city is relatively uncrowded, taken up mostly by processing desks and medical examination facilities. Some of the staff here are Westerners; I hear English and a few Scandinavian sounding exchanges. I walk by the food distribution centre. A couple of trucks filled with high stacks of bags of rice are backed up here, and the line-up of people waiting to receive their allocated ration snakes deep into the thicket of shelters. I ask one of the staff how much each person gets. It depends on what type of voucher they have, the young woman hollers back: adults 400 grams per day, children 150 grams. Some of the people lining up have vouchers for a whole family, she explains. The line-up is between six and eight hours long.

Apparently free to go wherever I want to, I walk past the outer periphery, into the next layer, and it's here that I encounter unimaginable scenes. The deeper I get into this miserable community, the worse it gets. Starving children lie around, bellies badly extended, some with parts of their faces covered with thick clusters of flies. Many of the adults look emaciated too, some uncontrollably crying, others laughing hysterically, then breaking down. There are mothers holding babies to their withered breasts, the babies too exhausted to suck. I see one mother collapsed on the ground, next to her dead toddler, hysterically sobbing.

I can't take it for long, this wretched display of human suffering. After an hour or so, I turn around, making my way back to the perimeter tents and chat up a young nurse. She's leaning against the side of a fencepost, smoking a cigarette. She's from Hungary, a member of a Soviet relief delegation, and she works at the processing desk. The stories of abuse and cruelty are unbelievable, she tells me—babies randomly bayonetted, women raped by whole groups of Pakistani soldiers, men loaded onto trucks to be taken to the nearest field and executed. She's convinced India will soon enter the war and it'll get even worse.

What I saw outside Calcutta that day in 1971 was a small part of the disaster that is now referred to as either the Bangladesh Genocide or the Bangladesh Liberation War, depending on perspective. The idealism and unreserved humanity of the exhausted camp volunteers I met that day left me stunned and imprinted me forever.

I travelled on afterwards, eastward through Asia at first, where I soon found myself amidst the chaos unleashed by the Vietnam War. Eventually, I crossed the ocean to settle in one of the world's most blessed places, Canada. It was as if the universe was rewarding me for my efforts to open my eyes and explore.

Much like my father, I struggled to make a living at first, but soon succeeded on a scale I could not have imagined. Within a few years, I earned what seemed to me enormous sums of money and, once a year at Christmas, gave a percentage of it away. I knew little about the organizations I supported, nor was I in touch with them or understood how exactly my donations were used.

What mattered was that I could write an ever-greater number of cheques. It made me feel incredibly good; I felt that the long hours I worked generated benefits not just for myself, but also the world outside. Giving money was even better than earning it—I felt I was making a difference.

Epiphany

**The Friday Visit
that Helped Me Understand**

Twenty or so years into my career, a remarkable thing happened. A lady from Doctors Without Borders called me. She said they'd noticed my steadily growing annual donations and were thankful for them. Would I like to come and visit, so that they could show me what my grants had accomplished?

It was a Friday when I arrived at the charity's offices; I know that because I remember feeling terribly sorry for myself. I'd had a rough week at work, one of the worst ever, with administrative entanglements and a lousy market leaving me exhausted.

Then, after being introduced to some key people, I met the logistics expert who directed the relief operations of which Canada's section was in charge. Sitting down in his tiny and heavily cluttered office, I casually asked how things were going. "Well," I was told, "it's been a difficult day." He vaguely pointed at the white-board on the wall behind him, where column headings referred to some of the most challenged places I could think of: Chechnya, the Nigerian Delta, Haiti, Somalia and half a dozen others—civil war theatres, refugee sanctuaries, hotbeds of disease, places where malnutrition and famine reigned. I asked my host to tell me more.

Sometimes, he explained, staff can move without constraint and help on a massive scale. But just as often, there is a population group, a military faction or a government that intervenes, blocking the mission's work or tyrannizing the victims seeking help. "There are moments when you come to accept abuse, beatings, and even loss of life as almost commonplace," he said. Then he told me about the abduction of a friend he'd been in the field with not long ago.

There are times in life when we need perspective and context, and this is what my first visit to Doctors Without Borders brought me. I was back where I'd been, seemingly a lifetime ago, when I visited the refugee camp. Not only did my work-related problems seem utterly trivial, but there was so much more. The man I'd met with had stayed long past his office hours taking time to explain, to open himself to me, to tell me about his ongoing struggle to come to terms with what he routinely experienced.

I felt humbled, yet so grateful. I'd just been taught how comparatively insignificant my contributions to society, humanity and the universe were.

I made it my business to regularly visit Doctors Without Borders. And each time I stopped by I learned more. Before long, my new friends became my heroines and heroes. Their work inspired me on a personal level, teaching me about commitment and focus, and what can be done when all seems hopeless. I also became intrigued with how well they managed an extremely complex operation. Having held executive positions in the financial industry and being overly familiar with financial analysis, I found myself baffled by how Doctors Without Borders could achieve unrivalled social impact while being run on an insanely disciplined budget.

Some of my newly gained insights came with regrets. As I studied the operational efficiencies of Doctors Without Borders, the weaknesses at other charities became woefully apparent. Some of the organizations I'd given money to turned out to be cash-hoarding machines, banking vast amounts of money and channelling only a small portion of donations to what their literature portrayed as causes in desperate need. Others had unacceptably high administrative costs, often aggravated by excessive management compensation. Then there was the issue of fundraising: did I want my donations to make a difference now, or would I prefer that my money be spent on pamphlets, advertisements and call centres? To be sure, soliciting donations can be an important component of running a charitable enterprise, but the scale has to be justifiable. Of the causes I had supported, a disturbingly large number were spending between 30% and 35% of donations on fundraising!

Clearly, I'd given a lot of money to undeserving organizations, and thus deprived the best-run charities of funds they could have used far more effectively. Doctors Without Borders was one of them, and in time my research brought me to others, some in completely different areas of charitable activity. Gradually, I learned to give better—to give in a more targeted and intelligent way, to give where I could make the biggest difference.

> *"There are three kicks in every dollar. One when you make it. One when you save it. One when you give it away. And the last is the biggest of all."* - William Allen White

What else is there to say? In sharing my experience and presenting my conclusions I hope to have made only one major point: if the intention behind your charitable giving is to help in the most effective way, carefully consider where your donations should go.

There are tools that can greatly facilitate your search for worthy candidates. A list of different Canadian and U.S. services follows in my end pages. For now, just let me say that Canada's Charity Intelligence is the best I have found so far. It ranks registered charities by accountability, financial transparency, social impact, its need for donations and other benchmarks.

No matter what country you live in and what service you will turn to, checking out its leading charity rating organizations will give you valuable insights. Its data and editorial comments can be invaluable when it comes to balancing your intention to give with incisive, up-to-date information.

Once you take a closer look, you'll be perplexed by what a small percentage of charities and non-profits deserve your support. But then again, you'll be even more surprised how much the worthiest organizations can accomplish!

The Many Faces of Charity

Frank's Approach
and Other Popular Delusions

The number of registered charities and non-profits is staggering. In Canada, there are some 86,000 registered charities and an additional 150,000 non-profit organizations. The U.S. tax authorities report over 1.5 million active registrants; worldwide, the number exceeds 10 million. Relatively few deserve your support.

I should also add that the difference between charities and non-profits is significant. In the Canadian context, a charity has to be of public benefit, is subjected to government oversight and can issue tax receipts for donations. Non-profit organizations have none of these regulatory requirements. In the United States, the distinction between the two is a bit more complicated.

Let me make an important point: throughout this guide, whenever I use the terms "a cause" or "an organization", I am referring to a registered charity. If you prefer to support not-for-profit entities, my document may be of limited use.

A few years ago, an elderly friend asked me to help him analyze what he called his 'charitable giving.' Let's call him Frank.

When I showed up at his place, Frank told me how blessed his life had been and what gratitude he felt. He invited me to sit down and handed me a handwritten two-page listing of the causes he favoured. There were only two columns, one showing the names of the organizations he had chosen, the other the dollar amounts allocated to them.

The largest bequest was to a local think tank, well known for its ardent political partisanship. I set up my laptop and showed Frank how to log into the website of Charity Navigator, a U.S. analytical service. It took me seconds to locate the CEO's annual salary: US$720,000, a figure I found highly offensive.

Right from the beginning we had two problems. The organization's stated engagement was not charity but politics, and the top operative was overly compensated. There were other red flags as well, but I left those aside. Instead I asked, "How much are you giving them each year?"

Frank seemed surprised. He explained that his list was to become effective only upon his death. His will was overdue for an update, which was why he'd asked me for help.

> *"Feeling gratitude and not expressing it is like wrapping a present and not giving it."* - William Arthur Ward

Curiosity welled up in me. "Why not give some of your money away now?" I asked, admittedly a bit too early in our dialogue. "I mean, you're worth many millions and have no descendants, and I'm sure you recognize there is much need for help out there now." Then I hastily added, "Plus, there may be a tax advantage. You could offset some of your current income by contributing now," thinking this might sway him. But it didn't. He made references to the possibility that, given his advanced age, he may require expensive medical treatment—better not to take that risk.

I couldn't stop myself. "Even if you get a two-million-dollar bill, that's still a small fraction of your net worth," I pointed out. And then I uttered the unimaginable: "Besides, if there is no risk involved, it's not really charity. All it is in your case is a hedge against estate taxes."

To his credit, my friend took my comment in stride and we returned to his list. Most of his chosen charities were household names. Only a few had an acceptable level of administration and fundraising costs and even fewer could be termed impactful.

Yet, each time I pointed to an inadequacy and suggested that the charity in question wasn't worthy, Frank responded with something like, "Well, I can't take them off my list. I knew the founder socially when I lived in New York. And we did business together." I felt tempted to add that corporate tit-for-tat wasn't really charity either, but this time I kept quiet.

When I left my friend's house, I realized that we'd changed almost nothing, something that rarely happens. I admired Frank in many ways, but what had just happened left me profoundly disappointed. Fortunately, when I help others analyze their charitable activities, the outcome is usually far more positive.

One thing I've learned is that the majority of large and small donors start out with serious misconceptions. The most common are these:

THE 'BIGGER IS BETTER' DELUSION

"I always stick to the top names. Large charities are large because they're doing things right."

My reaction:
Big brand marketing creates an impression of trustworthiness. Yet size rarely improves quality or efficiency—in any human endeavour. That is not to say that large charities can't be worthy. But a quick look at the data confirms that many of the best-known organizations spend an inordinate amount of their revenue on fundraising and administration, while convincingly broadcasting how urgent their appeal for help is. That, of course, is also the case with some smaller charities. Still, importantly, size does not make things better.

THE 'TIT-FOR-TAT IS NECESSARY' THEORY

"My peers in the corporate world did me a favour and now I'm reciprocating it. What can be wrong with that?"

My reaction:
There is no doubt that helping others brings rewards. But helping with the expectation of a reward strips your gesture of its moral weight. Let's say someone helped you and you now want to do something for them—that is a worthy gesture, but it shouldn't be a consideration when it comes to charitable giving. What you have to ask yourself is whether this is about an old relationship or whether it's about helping someone in indisputable need.

THE 'KIND UNCLE WILBERT' NOTION

"I like to honour the memory of the dead. When someone I respected dies from cancer, I send money to the Cancer Society. Besides, it's usually the charity the family favours—it says so in the obituary."

My reaction:

This emotion brings tens of millions into the coffers of national cancer societies, heart and stroke foundations and other health-oriented charities. The question is really this: are you favouring the recommended cause because it is a convenient and visible gesture towards the grieving family, or are you doing it because you believe in the cause's merits?

Sometimes my attempts to be of help evoke negative emotions. A frequent one is this: "Wait a minute—no one has the right to tell me who I should give my money to."

I'm never sure whether the energy in that comment is directed at me or people like Charity Intelligence, whose data I rely on. Nor does it matter. After all, it's natural to get strong reactions when you help someone take responsibility for their personal affairs.

My response is always the same: "True enough, only you can decide which cause you want to support. But doesn't it help when others offer their insights, so that you can make a good decision?"

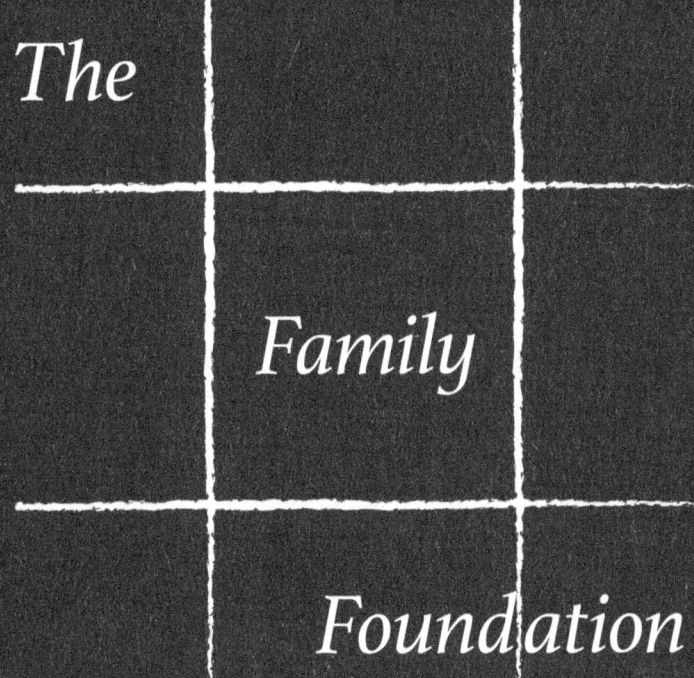

The Family Foundation

What I Learned from My Grandchildren

When I turned sixty, I decided to start a foundation. Having seen numerous wealthy clients pass away and leave money to charitable causes, I wondered whether I should do the same. For a couple of decades, I'd steadily given away ten percent of what I earned, but there was room for a lot more. Should I crank up the percentage now or copy what my clients did and leave a large bequest in my will? I decided on the former alternative: giving while living.

Taking the foundation approach was not my only option. I could easily have increased my giving without the added complication of an administrative structure. The reason I chose to start the Cavelti Family Foundation was simple: I was eager to create a legacy, ideally one that would stretch over generations, and even more importantly, I wanted to share my journey with my family.

I had two choices. One, I could establish a trust or a not-for-profit corporation and then apply to be registered as a charity. There were significant legal costs to that, and the process could take some time. Moreover, the ongoing operation of a registered charity would require the formation of a Board of Directors and bring with it a heavy and expensive administrative load. I was determined to avoid that.

The alternative was a way to delegate all the paperwork and regulatory burden to our city's community foundation. This would be done through a "Donor Advised Fund". For an annual fee, the Toronto Foundation would perform all necessary administrative tasks, invest undistributed funds and deal with tax authorities, allowing me to focus on what really mattered.

Still, I was hesitant. I understood that a community foundation's first objective was to help charitable activities within their town or city, and I could relate to that concept. But could I be sure that I'd agree with the Toronto Foundation's choices, and did I want to restrict our giving to causes within our city? The answer was no—I was determined that it should be our family that would decide where our grants would be directed.

Yet, after a couple of meetings I learned that the Toronto Foundation offered several granting alternatives for Donor Advised Funds. Importantly, we'd be able to decide which charitable causes we wanted to support and when. This was crucial to me.

Three years into the life of my foundation, I thought the time was right to involve the family. Not sure what would come out of it, I started by bringing all three grandchildren to my office, promising them a real business meeting and telling them I needed their help. They were excited.

"Do any of you know what charity is?" I started out. Alexandra, at twelve the eldest, told me that she'd participated in a fundraiser organized by her school. Cameron, in fourth grade, reported that some of the older kids in his neighbourhood had raised money by selling cookies.

"But what do you think the word 'charity' means?" I persisted. The youngest, Abigail, provided the answer. "That's easy, Papa. Charity means being kind." I was touched by the irresistible simplicity of her assessment, concluding that we were off to a good start.

At our second meeting, we discussed the complexities of giving money away. When I provided an overview of the different types of charities and asked how they felt about each, I was taken aback. I knew humanitarian relief organizations resonated with

Cameron and imagined that Doctors Without Borders would be on top of his list. I was right.

It was the girls' notion of who should benefit from our foundation that surprised me. Social initiatives or after-school programs left them unenthusiastic, and so did environmental initiatives. They wanted to help animals. I hadn't expected that.

As time went on their priorities changed. What made a meaningful difference was my exposing them to Charity Intelligence. I had feared that introducing them to sets of data would dampen their enthusiasm, but it did the opposite. Gradually their focus widened. The girls were still passionate about animal welfare and Cameron's heart was still close to Doctors Without Borders, which he now expertly called MSF for Médecins Sans Frontières. But sitting at one of our oversized computer screens and studying what happened to the donations that various charities received, focused them on new possibilities.

"Look Papa," one of the kids would exclaim, "here is a charity that pays way too much in salaries." Or, "I think I've found one we should support—nearly 80% goes to the cause!" How much of the money an organization collected was spent on actual charitable activities (as opposed to administration or fundraising) was one of their favourite metrics. Before long they produced elaborate spreadsheets, detailing each charity's merits and shortcomings.

Now was the time to talk about different ways of giving. One thing I was not prepared for was the extent of children's idealism. They quickly agreed that directly engaging with others was a much higher form of compassion than giving money away. The girls convinced themselves that they'd adopt lots of dogs and cats; Cameron's declared priority was to help people, especially the sick, disabled, and hungry.

But how would they do that? After I invited the children to seriously explore their goals, the conversation started to change. They could see that there were limitations to what was possible. To begin with, realities like school and parents would render their ideas hopelessly impractical. Maybe it was easier to collect money and send it to people who were already in the right places to provide help, with the time and knowledge to do what was needed. Our foundation, of course, attempted to do just that

The next step was to give each of the kids a small allocation they could grant to the causes of their choice. Questioning their decisions was always a highlight for me. Without exception, their decisions were well-researched. In time, I invited them along to meetings with groups we supported or considered adding to our list. By now I felt our foundation would be in good hands once I was gone.

> *"As I give, I get." - Mary McLeod Bethune*

Importantly, the grandchildren aren't the only ones who learned from their engagement. The family foundation has taught me a lot, too. I now realize that many of the skills I learned during my business career, particularly writing and public speaking, can be applied to purposes other than corporate success. Some charities call me for an informed outsider's opinion; others ask me for advice or invite me to address staff meetings or groups of high-level donors. Occasionally Kate Bahen, the Managing Director of Charity Intelligence, looks for input. Invariably, the outcome is as gratifying to me as it is beneficial to them.

Navigating the Charitable Map

Thoughts about Human Failures
and Hopes for a Better Future

What kind of cause resonates with you? If you'd asked me this question when I was in my forties, I would have given you an unequivocal answer: humanitarian relief. No doubt my sentiment was tinged by my backpacking trip through horribly impoverished areas of Africa and Asia.

But over time, I gained new perspectives. And my preferences continue to evolve. A big part of the ongoing changes in our granting patterns is related to top-down considerations. Some time ago, my daughter Melissa confided that she would never allocate the lion's share of our donations to Doctors Without Borders. Humanity seemed a failed experiment, she declared—much better to help distressed animals. I considered her position, but the miserable memories of the Bangladesh war victims I had been destined to see in my early twenties crowded out any images of rescue animals I could evoke.

My wife Caroline also affected the course of our giving. Why not spend more on "boosting human potential", she proposed. Without a more compassionate society, the suffering around the world would continue forever.

Before long, we all became less dogmatic and widened our scope. Caroline's input led me to the discovery of a superbly managed after-school program, "Beyond 3:30", which, in turn, focused me on educational initiatives as an obvious hope for the future of the human race. We started paying attention to other causes too, from food banks to clean water projects to social justice and environmental causes and, yes, animal welfare.

Bit by bit, our family foundation's granting allocations changed. Out of dozens of segments (from cancer research to homeless shelters, universities and veterans' support), we chose a handful that really resonated with us. Humanitarian relief still ranks high, but it now represents about a third of the causes we support—down from twice that much a few years ago.

Not long ago, I invited everyone in the family to tell me how they would allocate funds between the five segments we favour, without talking to each other. The responses were eerily similar and closely reflected the targets I had written down myself:

Humanitarian Relief (shelter, medical, food)	35%
Community, Education, Human Potential	35%
Animal Welfare	10%
Environment	10%
Better Giving (charity analysis)	10%

It seems that what we'd all learned is that there was an urgent need for help on more fronts than we could have imagined. The challenge now was to find the charities that could put our donations to work most efficiently.

There was another lesson we'd learned: supporting the "Better Giving" segment could produce extraordinary results. Why would we want to allocate 10% of our donations to something like charity analysis, we're often asked. The answer is quite simple: donor surveys reveal that the vast majority of users change their giving after reading charity reports. What that means to us is that supporting a good analysis service will cause thousands of others to abandon poorly run organizations and favour worthy ones.

Here are two fascinating charts from a study done in 2020 by a group of researchers. Max Roser of Our World In Data subsequently captured the results in visual form. The first illustration shows how most potential donors don't think that the effectiveness varies much between charities. Yet when the researchers asked renowned global experts, the results were dramatically different. The specialists, it turns out, feel that below-average charities don't accomplish much at all, and those to the very left of the graph actually harm people.

As you may have noted, this study targeted health related charities, but in my experience the difference between the poorly managed and efficiently run organizations is equally huge in every segment of the charitable universe.

How much do charities differ in terms of cost-effectiveness?

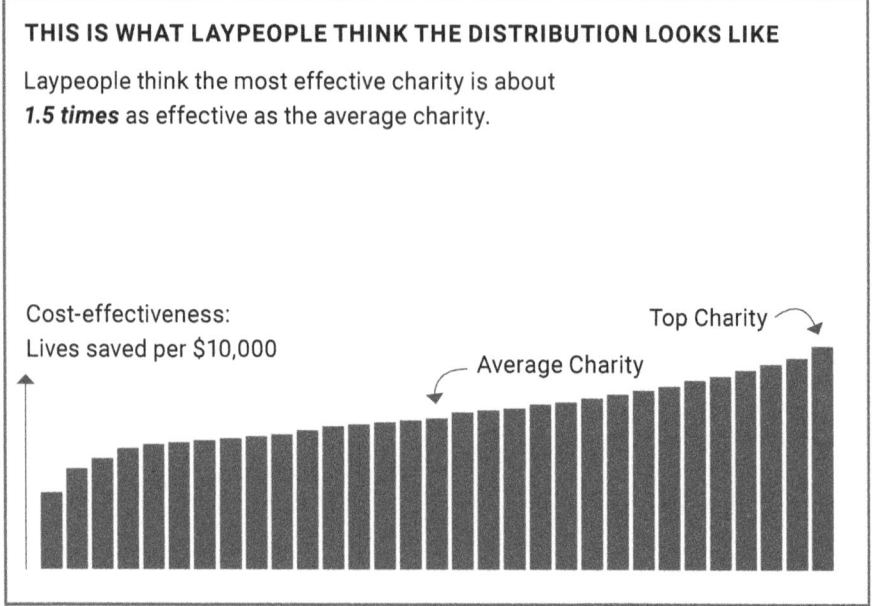

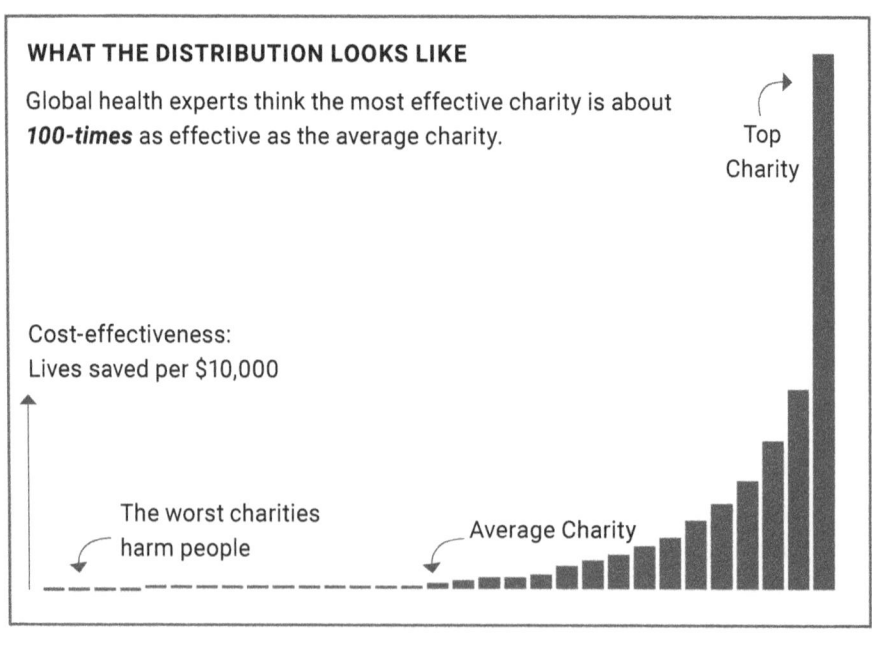

Do you have to become an expert to give better? No, but resorting to informed analysis helps a lot. Here are some data that from Charity Intelligence's 2022 survey that speak for themselves:

89% of respondents find that charity reporting informed their giving. Across all information categories donors find Charity Intelligence's research 'very useful'. 'Very useful' responses were three times higher than 'useful'.

70% of respondents change their giving after reading a charity report. Their giving changes to charities with higher impact and higher star ratings. Underlying this change, our impact scores have greater influence than the overall star rating.

Donors double the impact of their giving when their giving changes. In moving support away from charities with low or fair impact to charities with good or high impact, giving picks up in its social return on investment.

For the full survey, check the following link:

https://www.charityintelligence.ca/research-and-news/ci-views/33-donor-giving/735-2022-giving-insights-charity-intelligence-s-donor-survey-results

The question I keep asking myself: could it be that $1,000 given to Charity Intelligence could bring more money to one of our favourite causes than if we gave the same $1,000 directly to it? Let's assume that the charity in question had a five-star rating, which inspired thousands of donors to redirect their grants from two-star and three-star rated causes? Take another look at the charts above—if the most effective charity in a given segment is about 100 times as effective as the average charity, then the impact of such a shift in donor behaviour would be monumental!

Would it really work that way? I'll never know, but I believe it's a strong possibility. And that is why a 10% allocation to the charity analysis segment makes eminent sense to me.

The Good the Bad and the Ugly

Three Easy Steps to Avoid Supporting Zombie Charities

When I come across a charity that seems worthy, I usually take a three-step approach. I first compare it to its peers operating in the same segment, then take a close look at the organization's website and sometimes engage with its staff. Finally, I examine what the rating services have to say. And all along, I keep the following criteria on top of my mind:

IF DONATIONS DON'T GET TO THE CAUSE QUICKLY, THERE IS NO POINT IN GRANTING

In other words, the causes I support have a justifiable reserve fund/program spending ratio. Money that can be used for the charity's programs should not be sitting in the bank. Here are my preferences. On the one hand, I want to make sure that reserve funds should be able to cover at least six months of the organization's charitable work. On the other, if an organization has cash reserves more than 2.5 times its annual program expenditures, I stay away.

A HIGH STANDARD OF FINANCIAL ACCOUNTABILITY IS A MUST

Many years ago, as a young executive of a financial institution, I was the head of the charitable action committee. My fellow board members were in the habit of enthusiastically supporting political campaigns but had limited interest in charity. I decided to change that and convinced my peers that we should give away $100,000 once a year. So, every fall I sent out 500 letters informing the recipients that we might choose their cause for a serious donation—our top pick would get $50,000, while five others would each be granted $10,000. All we needed to enter them in our contest was a brief description of their merits and audited financial statements. The replies were gushing with praise for our initiative, but fewer than 10% were willing to share financial details.

Little has changed in the charitable universe, on their side or mine. In the U.S. and Britain, the regulators' websites feature each charity's audited financial statements. In Canada, they are not publicly disclosed and, sadly, many organizations still won't allow routine access to their financials. My view hasn't changed during the past 50 years: I still detest charities that don't share detailed and audited information, ideally on-line.

AVOID CHARITIES THAT HAVE EXCESSIVE ADMINISTRATIVE/FUNDRAISING COSTS

Of course, different organizations carry different administrative burdens, but in general the combined total should not exceed 30% of total revenues. If in doubt, I evaluate the results of several candidates operating in each segment. For example, comparing the administrative or fundraising expenses of local foodbanks may help in choosing the most worthy cause.

EXECUTIVE SALARIES SHOULD BE JUSTIFIABLE

As a rule, the size and complexity of an operation should be considered. Interestingly, I have found that excessive management compensation is more often a problem with small charities than with large ones. My advice: take a close look at salary levels and use your judgment.

IMPACT IS EVERYTHING

Arguably the most important measure of excellence is to achieve high impact. Just consider: even if money goes to the cause quickly, and administrative, fundraising and compensation costs are kept low (which are all measures of efficiency), is the charity you're supporting effective? Or expressed differently, what resources have been put into place to address a specific problem and what tangible results do they achieve?

Let me resort to a couple of real-life examples. A few years back we compared two charities devoted to the fight against malaria. We wanted to know how many mosquito nets could be delivered if we donated $1,000. The result of our analysis was stunning:

the first organization incurred a cost per net of over $60, while the second could do the same thing for just under $15.

More recently, we studied the results achieved by two programs designed to keep children in challenged neighbourhoods off the street during the critical hours between the end of the school-day and their parents' return home from work. Both charities did a reasonably good job keeping the kids occupied, but one ("Beyond 3:30", managed by the Toronto Foundation for Student Success) could demonstrate a considerable improvement in the grades of the children who were signed up for the program. That's the kind of outcome I want to see.

Measuring social impact is not only a key to choosing a deserving cause, but also one of the most challenging parts of a donor's homework. Fortunately, some of the better charity analysis services provide answers, although talking to the people inside the charity you are considering can provide you with additional insights.

> *"Life's most persistent and urgent question is: What are you doing for others?"* - Martin Luther King, Jr.

BEWARE OF "PHILANTHROPATHS"

I'm sure you've come across marketing messages or complimentary media coverage of charitable foundations founded by former politicians or corporate tycoons. Sometimes, such entities are worthy and even positively reviewed by rating agencies.

Yet, when digging a bit deeper and examining the origin of donations and where the grants go, we quickly learn that the intention behind some of these organizations is not charitable at all. Some engage in influence-peddling and political agitating, while others seem to be intent to change social or cultural dynamics. I've even come across examples where the charity was used to create business opportunities for the founder. I call such people "philanthropaths", and I'm sure most readers know of at least two or three figures who fall into this category.

Fortunately, the world has benefitted from the actions of true philanthropists, as well—people whose intentions were pure and whose commitment never wavered. In this context, I may as well mention Chuck Feeney, who made a fortune as the founder of the world's largest duty-free retail chain. By the late 1980s, as the financial press described him as the twenty-fourth richest American, Feeney had quietly transferred his wealth to his foundation, Atlantic Philanthropies, anonymously funding worthy charitable causes in the U.S. and around the world. By the time Feeney died in 2023, his charity had given away all its funds and closed its doors, having disbursed more than US$8 billion.

ONE MORE TIME: USE THE THREE-STEP APPROACH

Let me end this chapter with a word of caution. Some of the criteria I've mentioned lend themselves to an absolutist assessment. For example, if a charity can't get donations to the cause in an expedient manner or if it suppresses financial information, then yes, you have every reason to be critical. Another essential element is that we want to see demonstrable social impact. Yet, when it comes to other metrics, such as administrative costs or salaries, it can get more complicated. After all, things like staffing requirements, building maintenance or communications expenses vary enormously between a symphony orchestra, an animal shelter and a hospital.

That is why, as I mentioned above, I recommend you take three important steps when first considering a donation:

- **Compare the charity to others that are active in the same segment**—i.e., a food bank should be compared to another food bank.

- **Learn about the organization on its website,** which should feature all relevant information. If you need to inquire further, engage with the staff. Well managed charities welcome your questions.

- **Check what the analysts have to say,** but be aware that most rating services focus their research on large and medium-sized organizations. That means many well-run small charities aren't covered. In that case, the government operated websites can give you most of the details you need. (see our Annex on page 91).

Over the years, I've found that this methodology allows me to form a balanced and informed view.

How Many Causes Should We Support

Why We Cut the Number of Favoured Charities

For most of us, the practice of charitable giving is not something that follows a defined set of rules, but rather something that continuously evolves.

Before I started our family foundation, I supported no more than two charities. Once we operated through a larger platform that changed. Before long, we had a dozen or more organizations with whom we were "getting our toes wet", and as many that we were committed to, but which weren't among our top choices. Then, in each segment we supported a "star charity" who received a more meaningful grant.

Why such complexity? I confess I can't think of any one compelling reason. Perhaps it's my intellectual curiosity which led me down this path, or maybe it was my background in investment management, where diversification is a guiding principle. Quite likely, the fact that each of our family members had different preferences contributed as well.

Either way, after a few years we decided to move toward a simplified model, which looks like this:

- We support no more than ten charities, whose work and practices we are very familiar with.

- In each of the five segments we focus on, at least 50% goes to our top pick.

- If we come across a previously unknown charity that intrigues us, we typically allocate a small amount to it and learn what we can through our experience with them.

I'm frequently asked whether it's even necessary to "diversify" when it comes to your giving. I firmly believe that it's not, although granting to two or three causes can provide you with more study material and allow you learn from comparing results.

Here is another consideration. If you donate as an individual or are the sole decision maker in the context of a foundation, giving all to one charity can make complete sense. If you run a family foundation and want others involved, it gets more complicated.

As individual donors or family foundations evolve, so do charities. The environment in which they operate changes, as does the leadership. During my four decades in the charitable arena I've seen committed idealist leaders replaced by dull technocrats, and I've witnessed the opposite. One persistent problem is that many sizeable organizations deliberately recruit corporate executives to their board, both due to the "tit-for-tat" principle and the need for administrative skills. That can seriously subvert charitable ethics. On the other hand, once a charity reaches a certain size, the kind of governance skills required are usually not met by idealism alone.

Keeping a close eye on the causes you support is key. Be proactive in making connections within the charity, be inquisitive, and if needed be bold in your criticism. Like all institutional constructs, charities learn as much from listening to informed outsiders as from their own interpretation of the failures and successes they undergo.

Operating Charities and Public Foundations

Why Do I Need an Intermediary?

Few donors realize that there are "operating charities" and others which are often referred to as "public foundations". The difference is material.

As the Canada Revenue Agency sets it forth quite clearly, "Registered charities are allowed to operate in two ways: (1) by carrying their own activities, and (2) by giving resources to qualified donees", which include other registered charities.

So, what is a public foundation? It's an entity that does not directly engage in a given activity but distributes your donations to one or several other charities. It is, in simple terms, an intermediary.

I never took an in-depth look at this reality until the Covid pandemic hit. Due to the lockdowns and inflation caused by supply chain problems, large numbers of people ended up with food challenges. We decided to allocate a percentage of our grants to food banks.

Once I got to know the sector, I realized that some organizations never acquired or distributed any food. Their charity model was arranged around logistical and administrative knowhow—they were collecting money and passing it on to operating local food banks. Now I had a new problem. I'd long learned that in every segment of charity (as in every manifestation of human activity) there are a few organizations that excel, a more sizeable number that deserve a passing grade, and quite a few that consistently disappoint. Applying this principle to food banks, was I now supporting mediocrity?

In talking to the public foundations (or as I like to call them, intermediaries) I first learned that their main talent is to make the donating public aware of a given need, which from the perspective of the local operators who usually lack marketing skills, is of immense advantage. There was nothing negative about that.

But when I examined the granting done by these intermediaries, the negatives became more discernible. One of the humanitarian relief charities prided itself as giving 81% of donations to the cause. What that meant was that the intermediary organization spent 19% on administration and fundraising expenses before passing the rest on to the operating charities. A closer look revealed that among the dozen or so sizeable charities receiving funding, several had unacceptably high administrative and fundraising ratios of their own, and some achieved notoriously low impact.

Many donors favour intermediary organizations, because they make giving to a variety of 'good causes' so simple. The problem, of course, is that some of the supported causes may not be good at all. In other words, donors believe that the intermediary ensures that its favoured charities are efficient, accountable and achieve high social impact, but that assumption is often tragically wrong.

Here is how we dealt with this problem. We contacted the public foundations that we felt were enabling unworthy causes and informed them that we could no longer help them. Instead, we explained, our grants would go directly to one or two of the worthiest operating charities they had supported. Why, after all, would we want to donate through an intermediary, which had its own set of expenses. They didn't like that but found it hard to argue against it.

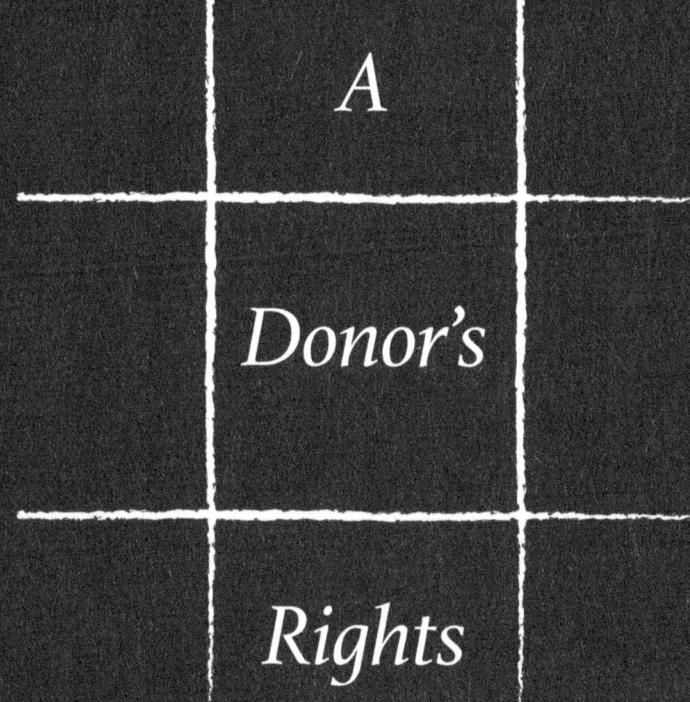

**Honouring a Donor's Rights
Means Being Accountable**

What rights does a donor have? Unfortunately, there is no easy answer to that. In the end, your enthusiasm for a cause and how much you think of an organization will determine the degree of your support.

Still, there are charities that distinguish themselves by posting their policies and their underlying ideologies, a practice that resonates with me. Some precede the specific donor's rights they have adopted with this statement crafted three decades ago by a group of charitable advisory associations:

"Philanthropy is based on voluntary action for the common good. It is a tradition of giving and sharing that is primary to the quality of life. To assure that philanthropy merits the respect and trust of the general public, and that donors and prospective donors can have full confidence in the not-for-profit organizations and causes they are asked to support, we declare that all donors have these rights..."

Among the rights listed are a few obvious ones, such as access for all to information about the way donations are used, the identity of those determining policy, detailed financial statements and a pledge that grants will be used for the purposes they were given.

But then the list goes on, delving into promises that are more controversial. One of these is to acknowledge and recognize donors. This is an area where conventions widely differ. I think most people would agree that philanthropy represents an exchange of energy, one of the most profound transactions in human existence. The donor recognizes the worthiness of a cause and acknowledges the help of the volunteers and staff who help make a difference. Conversely, it would seem, the charity should recognize the donor's gesture of support.

Yet logistically, donor recognition presents challenges. For a small charity, it's demonstrably much easier to recognize its couple of hundred supporters than it is for a large organization with many thousands of donors. Some entities, to overcome this challenge, recognize only sizeable givers, organizing them into categories; the proverbial "platinum, gold and silver supporters" come to mind. Even within charitable organizations there is debate about what is right; Doctors Without Borders in Switzerland lists sizable supporters; the Canadian chapter opts not to do that.

As a donor, you should also be aware that marketing agencies routinely harvest donation data, such as your name and the size of your grant, from various charities' annual reports. They then sell this information to other charitable organizations. In short, being recognized as a donor with one charity can make you a fundraising target with another organization.

Another persistently controversial issue is whether a donor should be able to earmark funds to a specific cause. What if I feel that I'd like to help victims of the Sudanese civil war, but don't want my donation directed at mass Covid vaccination in Nepal? Should the charity of my choice observe such preferences? My own feeling is that they should, but realistically much depends on the size of your grant. After all, a charity may be able to direct a sizeable donation but will not be able to do the same for amounts of $500 or $1000. That is an ethical dilemma of the first order, but perhaps an insurmountable one.

Here is one of the more interesting donor rights, observed by very few charities: should a charity have to disclose whether those seeking donations are volunteers, employees of the organization, or hired solicitors? Almost all large charities retain marketing agencies who routinely pose as idealistic volunteer fundraisers but are paid handsomely for donors they bring to the table. That, to me, borders on the immoral.

And, finally, there is always the issue of selling the names of those who once supported the charity, but no longer do so. The small charity I mentioned covers that base too. It lists among its donor rights "to have the opportunity for their names to be deleted from our mailing list and to know that our charity will never share lists with others."

A few organizations even go further; they have privacy policies, complaints policies and even whistleblower policies in place.

To me, whether a charity has an accessible list of donor rights tells a lot about its ethics. And that is highly relevant, because an ethically deficient charity should neither be supported, nor call itself a charitable cause.

Balancing Intention with Thought

Back to Basics: the Challenge Is to Give Well

In sharing my experience and presenting my conclusions I hope to have made only one major point: if the intention behind your charitable giving is to help in the most effective way, carefully consider where your donations should go. There are numerous organizations in many areas of charitable activity whose work is admirable and whose social impact is impressive. Finding them and continuously reassessing their progress requires a bit of work but is also deeply rewarding. A disciplined review process will give you the time and distance that is needed for all successful decision making.

As you weigh the merits of each donation, you'll be perplexed by what a small percentage of charities and non-profits out there deserve your support. You'll be even more surprised how much the worthiest organizations can accomplish and what a difference your support can make!

> *"The greatest use of money is to spend it on something that will outlast your life." - Anonymous*

A LIST OF USEFUL CHARITY ANALYSIS SERVICES

Country	Source	Website	My Comments
Canada	Charity Intelligence	charityintelligence.ca	Best in class! In-depth analysis of roughly 800 charities, which represent 57% of total Canadian giving. Easily accessible, reliable data.
	Canada Revenue Agency	https://apps.cra-arc.gc.ca/ebci/hacc/srch/pub/dsplyBscSrch?request_locale=en	No recommendations, just solid facts on all registered charities.
	Charity Data / Blumbergs	charitydata.ca	Excellent. Detailed access to the most relevant metrics for a large number of charities.
	Smart Giving/ Blumbergs	smartgiving.ca	Tips on good giving, avoiding scams.

Country	Source	Website	My Comments
USA	Charity Navigator	http://charitynavigator.org/	Key data points for roughly 200,000 charities. Risk: such broad coverage can limit depth of analysis.
	Charity Watch	charitywatch.org	Key data points, but smaller coverage.
	Give	give.org	Key data points, but smaller coverage.
	Guidestar	guidestar.org	Free overview, but detailed data require subscription.
	Give Well	http://givewell.org/	Raises funds and channels them to favoured charities, based on its research.

Please note that these organizations are typically registered charities themselves. While they make most of their information available for free, they depend on donations to keep operating.

A LIST OF INSIGHTFUL EDUCATIONAL ARTICLES

https://www.mulagofoundation.org/blogs/making-ourselves-accountable

"We think that funders like us should be accountable for impact, just like investors are accountable for profit. Without that we - philanthropy and aid - will only accomplish a fraction of what we might have. This is an effort to get out ahead and put our money where our mouth is." A brilliant summation by Mulago Foundation's self-critical CEO, Kevin Starr.

https://www.mulagofoundation.org/articles/dont-feed-the-zombies

Kevin Starr at it again. This time he explains how he used to blame ineffective charitable organizations, wondering why they didn't work harder, smarter, but how we, the donors are culprits too. "Money is the lifeblood of social sector organizations, we are the ones who allocate it, and we are the least accountable in the whole system. If there are zombies roaming the landscape, it's on us." Must read.

https://denver-frederick.com/2021/07/28/mulago-foundation-ceo-on-mission-impact-scaling-and-more/

An entertaining and educational conversation between Kevin Starr, the CEO of the Mulago Foundation, and Denver Frederick, the Host of The Business of Giving.

https://www.atlanticphilanthropies.org/lessons-learned-the-harvest-time-reports

Atlantic Philanthropies was the largest endowed institution to put all its charitable assets to use in a fixed period of time and then close its doors. In 2010, it commissioned consultant Tony Proscio, in conjunction with Duke University Center for Strategic Philanthropy & Civil Society, to write a series of reports charting the final years of the foundation. These seven reports examine the major decisions made behind concluding operations and the culminating "big bets". Highly insightful; recommended for advanced students of the charitable universe. (See my comments on Chuck Feeney, the founder of Atlantic Philanthropies, in the chapter "The Good, The Bad And The Ugly").

"The Billionaire Who Wasn't: How Chuck Feeney Secretly Made and Gave Away a Fortune", by Connor O'Clery. The definitive book on Chuck Feeney's remarkable philanthropic journey. Available in book stores, as well as Amazon, Goodreads and other websites.

https://cavelti.com/causes-we-support/

At the Cavelti Family Foundation, half of the causes we support fall into the "small" category. Charities with a smaller footprint typically get less media coverage and are often better managed and more attuned to the needs of their constituencies. Large or small, we are proud to share who the major recipients of our grants are. Our webpage also explains why we feel they deserve our help.

Acknowledgements

First, I want to thank my wife Caroline, my daughter Melissa and my grandchildren Alexandra, Cameron and Abigail for joining me on my journey through the charitable universe.

I'd also like to acknowledge the readers of various drafts of this manuscript, whose comments and suggestions are much appreciated. Special thanks go to Kate Bahen of Charity Intelligence and to Kathryn Sutton. Also, this guide wouldn't be complete without Richard Moore's design input and Minh Nguyen's thoughtful work on layout and content.

And finally, I want to acknowledge the many insights I've been offered and lessons I've been taught during the decades of my charitable engagement. Some were in response to my questions and others came unsolicited. Some were offered with kindness and the noblest intentions, while others were driven by greed and sometimes cynicism. But I've learned from them all and feel privileged to keep passing on the knowledge I have gained.

Toronto, Spring 2024

Also by Peter C. Cavelti

TUIAVII'S WAY:
A SOUTH SEA CHIEF'S COMMENTS ON WESTERN SOCIETY

Tuiavii, a young Chief in early 20th century Samoa, reveres the white man and his message of love. After all, haven't the missionaries taught his people to put down their weapons, honor one another and live in harmony? To visit Europe and learn its ways becomes Tuiavii's burning desire.

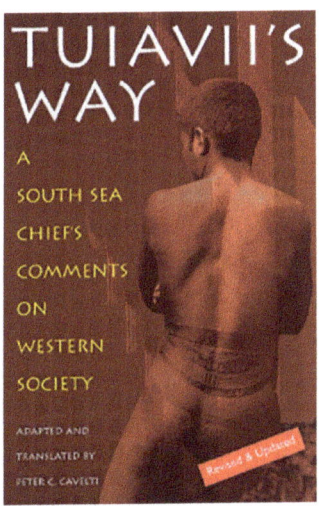

But once he arrives on the continent as part of a traveling show, he quickly becomes disillusioned. What Tuiavii witnesses is not the life of sharing and love he expected, but one in which greed, haste and hypocrisy dominate. Now he must find a way to return home and warn his people.

As delightful in their simplicity as they are prescient, Chief Tuiavii's comments confer the ultimate gift—the ability to see ourselves through another culture's eyes and, in turn, understand ourselves better. As we read on, we are saddened by the loss of simplicity and humanity in our society. In his masterful English translation, Peter C. Cavelti offers us Tuiavii's enduring wisdom along with a compelling cultural perspective.

A fascinating and all too rare look at ourselves through another culture's eyes. Editor's Choice!
Ottawa Citizen

Profound and prescient, written from an innocent, yet enchanting perspective. Publishers Group West

Recommended reading: a true eye-opener for all travellers to Down Under. DoAustralia.com – Australia's Tourism Website

A must read for any student of comparative culture and anthropology.
Roger Plunk, Author of "America's Highest Destiny"

[Purchase on Amazon](#)

Published 1997 by Gutter Press in Canada;
1999, 2007 and 2020 by Legacy Press in the U.S. and Canada;
2008 and 2024 by Sanseido Publishing in Japan.